D1143282

A Dorling Kindersley Book

Project Editor Linda Martin
Art Editor Peter Bailey
Designer Mark Regardsoe
Photography Pete Gardner

First published in Great Britain in 1991 by Dorling Kindersley
Publishers Limited, 9 Henrietta Street, London WC2E 8PS

**A CIP catalogue record for this book is available
from the British Library**

ISBN 0-86318-587-8

Reproduced in Hong Kong by Bright Arts
Printed in Belgium by Proost

MY SCIENCE BOOK OF GROWTH

Written by
Neil Ardley

Dorling Kindersley • London

What is growth?

Growth means getting bigger. All living things grow by taking in food. You grow because you are a living thing and because you eat food. The food you eat is in the form of plants, or animals that eat plants. But what do plants "eat"? Green plants make their own food from air, water and sunlight. Plants use this food to grow stems and leaves, and sometimes flowers and fruits. Trees that start life as tiny seeds can grow as tall as houses, or even taller.

A world of life
All life on Earth depends on the growth of plants. Plants make much of the oxygen that people and animals need to live.

Water your plants
Plants need water to live. Without water they will stop growing and die.

Useful plants
This boy's sweatshirt is made of cotton, which comes from a tropical plant. The paper pages of the book he is reading are made from wood fibres from trees.

Greatest growth

Sequoia trees are the biggest living things in the world. They can grow as high as 110 metres. As it grows from a seed, a tree like this increases its weight about a million, million times!

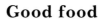

Good food

Fruits and vegetables are healthy foods that come from plants. Many foods that help us to grow, such as bread and sugar, are made from plants.

⚠ This sign means **take care**. You should ask an adult to help you with this step of the experiment.

Be a safe scientist
Follow all the directions carefully and always take care, especially with glass, scissors, matches, candles, and electricity.

Never put anything into your ears, mouth or eyes. If you do not want to waste the seedlings you have grown, you can plant them in pots or in a garden.

Getting growing

How do plants begin life and grow? Many grow from seeds formed by parent plants. A bean is the seed of a bean plant. See what happens when a bean begins to grow, or "germinate", into a new bean plant.

You will need:

Tall glass jar

Jug of water

Paper towels

Bowl of water

Runner bean seeds

1 Soak a few beans in water overnight.

2 Roll up several paper towels. Put them in the jar.

3 Put a bean between the paper and the side of the jar. You can put about four beans in the jar if you want to.

The paper towels soak up the water.

4 Add enough water to the jar to moisten the paper towels. Leave the jar in a warm place.

5 After about two days, a tiny root pushes its way through the bean's hard outer skin.

Add water to keep the paper moist.

A seed contains the food that the new seedling needs to grow.

Now that the new plant has leaves, it can make its own food (see p.23).

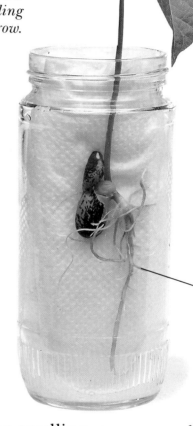

6 Over the next two days, the root grows downwards and a shoot starts to push its way out of the bean.

The shoot grows up, looking for light.

Tiny roots have grown from the main root.

The root grows down, looking for water.

7 The seedling, or young plant, continues to grow very fast. After ten days, the shoot has become a leafy stem.

Sowing seeds
This farmer is scattering seeds in a field. If the conditions are right, the seeds will germinate and grow into new plants where they fall.

Seed needs

What makes a seed begin to germinate? By growing your own seeds, you will discover that if they have water, oxygen from the air, and warmth, they will soon start to grow into new plants.

You will need:

Three deep saucers

Jug of water

Mung bean seeds

Bowl of water

Paper towels

1 Soak the beans in water overnight. Drain and rinse them.

2 Put several paper towels in each saucer.

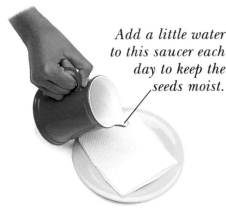

Add a little water to this saucer each day to keep the seeds moist.

3 Pour enough water into the first saucer to moisten the paper towels.

4 Scatter beans on to the paper in all three saucers.

5 Gently fill the second saucer with water. Make sure that the beans are completely covered.

Add water every day to this saucer as well.

The dry beans do not germinate at all.

6 Leave the saucers somewhere warm for about five days. The three sets of beans will look quite different.

These beans germinate and grow into young Mung bean seedlings as they take in water and oxygen.

The beans under water begin to germinate. But they do not have enough air, and growth soon stops.

Watering crops
Seeds need water in order to germinate, and plants need water to stay alive. In areas where there is not much rain, farmers have to water their crops to prevent them from dying. This is called irrigation.

Growing in the dark

Do seeds need light to begin growing? You can find out by trying to grow some of your own at home in the dark.

You will need:

Mustard seeds

Lid or dish

Paper towels

Jug of water

Large cup

1 Fold a moist paper towel and put it in the lid.

2 Gently sprinkle some seeds on the paper.

3 Cover the seeds with the cup to keep out the light. Leave them in a warm place.

Check the seeds daily to see if they need more water. The paper towel should always be moist.

Growth after about six days

4 The seeds germinate and begin to grow, even though they are in the dark. The seedlings now need light and will die without it.

Spring bulbs

We plant bulbs in holes in the soil. Their roots grow down deep into the earth before the first shoots appear in search of light.

Too cold to grow

Why is it that plants never grow on cold, snowy mountain tops? You can find out by trying to grow seeds in the cold.

You will need:

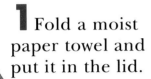

Mustard seeds

Lid or dish

Paper towels

Jug of water

1 Fold a moist paper towel and put it in the lid.

2 Gently sprinkle some seeds on the paper.

Make sure you keep the seeds moist.

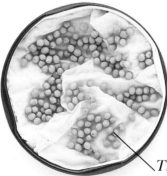

4 The cold seeds do not shoot. They need warmth in order to germinate.

The seeds look just the same as when you put them in the refrigerator.

3 Put the seeds in a refrigerator. Leave them for a few days.

Icy wasteland

Seeds need a certain amount of warmth in order to germinate. There are no plants to be seen here in Antarctica. It is much too cold all year round for them to grow.

Plant maze

Make a bean plant find its way through a maze! It will show you that a plant needs light as it grows. The plant uses light to make its own food once the food store in its seed has been used up.

You will need:

Two pieces of card

Pot of compost

Cardboard box

Scissors

Jug of water

Runner bean seed (soaked overnight)

1 Cut a large window in one end of the box.

2 Cut a window in each piece of card.

3 Plant the bean in the pot of compost. Water it well.

4 Stand the box upright and fit one piece of card a third of the way up the box. Put the pot in the bottom of the box.

The window in the card should be on the opposite side to the pot.

14

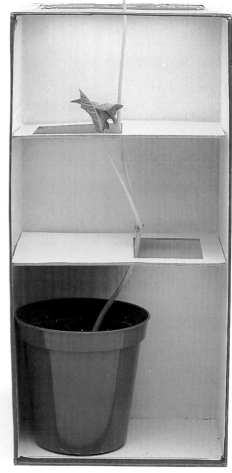

The seedling has grown towards the light coming down through the window.

5 Put the lid on the box and stand it in a light, warm place. Keep the bean moist.

Again, the window in the card should be away from the seedling.

6 When the seedling has grown through the first window, put the second shelf in.

7 The seedling changes direction again. It grows through the windows in the maze towards the light.

Tall trees
The trees in this forest grow to a great height to reach the light. Each tree tries to grow taller than the next tree to make sure it gets enough light. Trees need light to make food.

Brilliant bean

Can a seed tell the difference between up and down? Turn some growing beans upside-down to see how they are affected by "gravity".

You will need:

Jug of water

Paper towels

Bowl of water

Glass jar with lid

Two runner bean seeds

It does not matter which way the beans are pointing.

1 Soak the beans overnight. Crumple up some moist paper towels and put them in the jar. Add the beans.

Make sure you keep the paper moist.

2 After three or four days, roots start to grow down. A shoot pushes its way out of the bean.

The shoot turns to grow up in search of light. It grows against gravity.

3 When the roots are about 3 cm long, screw the lid firmly on the jar and turn it upside-down.

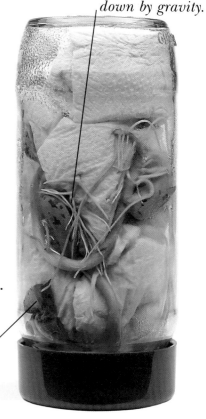

The roots turn so that they continue to grow down. They are pulled down by gravity.

4 Three to four days later, the roots and shoots have changed direction!

Clever carrot

Did you know that when you eat a carrot, you are actually eating the root of a carrot plant? You can grow a new carrot plant from a piece of carrot to see how clever this root is!

You will need:

Young, uncooked carrot

Saucer

Jug of water

Knife

1 ⚠ Ask an adult to cut off the top 3 cm of the carrot.

Add more water when the level falls.

2 Put the carrot top in a saucer and pour some water around it. Keep the saucer in a warm, light place for a week.

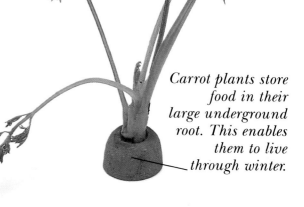

Carrot plants store food in their large underground root. This enables them to live through winter.

3 The carrot top grows new leaves! You can also grow parsnips, beetroots, and turnips in this way.

Plants from pieces

Do new plants only grow from seeds? You can find out by taking a "cutting" – a small piece of a plant that can produce its own roots and grow into a whole new plant.

You will need:

Rubber band

Secateurs

Fully grown geranium plant

Pot of moist compost

Clear plastic bag

Leaf joint

1 ⚠ Find a strong, young shoot without any flowers. Ask an adult to cut it off below a leaf joint.

Remove the lower leaves from the shoot before planting.

The shoot should be about 8cm long.

2 Make a hole in the moist soil and plant the cutting in it.

Remove the bag when the cutting starts growing. You will now need to water it regularly.

Secure the bag with a rubber band.

3 Put the bag over the cutting. Leave the pot in a warm place, out of direct sunlight.

The cutting grows its own roots. These take up water and minerals from the compost.

4 The cutting grows into a new geranium plant. This takes about six weeks.

Spreading strawberries

Strawberry plants make little plants without using seeds. Each parent plant grows special stems called "runners". You can use these to grow lots of strawberry plants!

You will need:

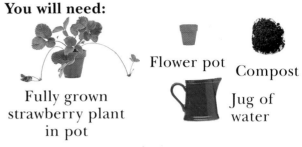

Fully grown strawberry plant in pot

Flower pot

Compost

Jug of water

1 Carefully fill the flower pot with compost.

Runner

Plantlet

2 Find a runner on the parent plant that has plantlets growing on it. Plant one of these in the pot. Water it well.

Leave the runner attached to the plantlet.

This runner will eventually wither away.

3 Over several weeks, the plantlet puts down its own roots and grows into a new strawberry plant. Soon the new plant sends out its own runners.

Root power

Plants send down roots through the soil to search for the water they need to live and grow. The roots also take up minerals, which help plants to grow. Roots are so strong that they can push their way through hard ground in their search for water. They can even break things!

You will need:

Half-eggshell

Egg cup

Marigold seeds

Jug of water

Compost

Saucer

Spoon

1 Carefully fill the half-eggshell with compost.

2 Put the eggshell in the egg cup. Sprinkle the seeds over the compost.

3 Put the egg cup on the saucer. Cover the seeds with a little compost.

4 Keep the egg–shell in a warm, light place. Water the compost lightly every day.

Do not let the compost get soggy.

The marigold plants shoot up towards to the light.

5 The seeds germinate after a few days and shoots appear. Leave them to grow.

6 About five weeks later, the eggshell begins to crack! The roots of the marigold plants push their way through the eggshell.

The roots continue to grow in their search for more water and minerals for the growing plants.

Stone breakers
Paving stones around trees are quite often lifted. Sometimes they are cracked. The roots of the trees are so strong that they can push up under the stones and damage them.

Thirsty flower

How much water does a plant need to stay fresh and alive? By giving a flower coloured water, you will see how good plants are at sucking up water through their stems.

You will need:

Fresh, white flower

Rubber band

Narrow vase of water

Cooking oil

Food colouring or ink

1 Add several drops of food colouring to the vase of water.

2 Gently pour the oil onto the water. Put the rubber band around the vase.

The oil floats on top of the water. It stops any water escaping into the air.

3 Put the flower in the vase. Move the rubber band so that it marks the top of the oil.

The water has travelled up the stem to the petals.

4 Leave the flower in a warm place for about two days.

The flower has sucked up this much water.

Desert plants
Cacti are able to live in dry deserts. They store the water that they take up from the soil.

Bubbling plant

How do green plants make the food they need to grow? They take in water and carbon dioxide, and use sunlight to change them into food. This process is called "photosynthesis". You can show how it also releases oxygen.

You will need:

Bowl of water

Jug of water

Jar

Card

Pond weed

Fill the jar to the top.

1 Put the pond weed in the jar. Fill it right to the top with water.

Make sure that no air gets into the jar.

2 Hold the card over the top of the jar. Turn the jar over and sub-merge it in the bowl. Remove the card.

The bubbles are oxygen. It forms when water and carbon dioxide, which is in air or water, are changed into food.

3 Put the jar where it will get plenty of light.

4 Bubbles appear on the leaves of the pond weed, and rise to the top of the jar.

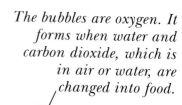

Indoor garden

How would you like to have your own indoor garden? You don't need much space because you can make it in a plastic or glass jar. Your plants will have everything they need to live and grow inside the jar.

You will need:

Spoon

Large jar with lid

Small pebbles Charcoal Compost

Water sprayer

Small plants

The pebbles help to drain the compost.

1 Lay the jar on its side. Cover the bottom with a layer of pebbles.

The charcoal keeps the water pure.

2 Next, cover the pebbles with a layer of charcoal.

3 Using the spoon, add a layer of compost.

4 Make some holes in the compost. Firmly press the roots of each plant into a hole.

5 When everything is in place, spray two or three squirts of water over the plants.

If there are no drops of water on the inside of your jar the next day, spray more water inside.

If water drops completely cover the inside of the jar, leave it open for a day.

The plants have the water, air, light, and warmth they need to grow.

6 Put the lid on and leave your indoor garden in a warm, light place where there is no direct sunlight.

Growing under glass

Plants grow well in greenhouses. The glass walls shelter the plants from the cold, but allow the Sun's rays to provide them with the light and warmth they need to grow.

Yeast feast

Have fun with some yeast, which is a very simple kind of plant called a "fungus". Fungi cannot make their own food like green plants, so they need to be fed. By giving yeast some sugar, you can make it blow up a balloon!

You will need:

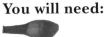
Balloon

150 ml warm water

Narrow-necked bottle

Three teaspoons yeast

Two teaspoons sugar

1 Put the yeast and sugar in the bottle. Gently pour in the warm water.

2 Put the neck of the balloon firmly over the bottle.

3 Over the next few hours, the balloon slowly blows up as the liquid in the bottle goes frothy.

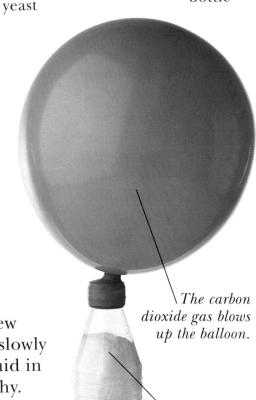

The carbon dioxide gas blows up the balloon.

As the yeast feeds on the sugar, it produces bubbles of carbon dioxide.

Bread–making
Yeast is used to make bread. Carbon dioxide gas, from yeast mixed with sugar, makes the dough rise before it is baked.

Spore print

Fungi, such as mushrooms, do not have seeds, so how do they grow? Make some "spore" prints to see how spores drop from mushrooms. These float through the air before they land and grow into new mushrooms.

You will need:

Flat mushrooms with dark undersides

Paper

1 Remove the stalks and put the mush-rooms on the paper. Leave them for a day or two.

The patterns are made by tiny, dust-like spores that fall from the underneath of each mushroom.

2 Carefully lift the mushrooms. Each one has produced a pattern of dark powder on the paper.

Puffing plant
Puffballs are also kinds of fungi. They puff out clouds of spores when rain falls on them. These spores are then carried through the air, and may grow into new puffballs where they land.

Magic mould

Make some mould, which is another kind of "fungus". It grows where mould spores land and find food, moisture and warmth.

You will need:

Jug of water

Antiseptic disinfectant

Plastic or glass container

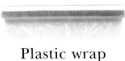
Plastic wrap

Three pieces of bread

1 You will need two pieces of fresh bread, and one piece of dry bread.

2 Moisten one piece of fresh bread with a little water.

3 ⚠ Ask an adult to pour a little disinfectant over the second piece of fresh bread.

Place the two pieces of bread as far apart as possible.

Keep the dry piece of bread outside.

4 Put these two pieces of bread in the container. Cover it with plastic wrap, and leave it in a warm place for several days.

Dry bread

Disinfected bread

Moist bread

5 After three days, mould begins to grow on the moist piece of bread. The dry bread and bread with disinfectant have no mould.

6 A few days later, the mould on the moist bread has grown quickly! How does the other bread look?

The disinfectant kills the spores so no mould grows.

New mould spores

Mould has started to grow where there is a little moisture left in the dry bread.

Moisture and warmth help the mould to feed on the bread so that the mould grows.

Picture credits
(Abbreviation key: B=below, C=centre, L=left, R=right, T=top)

The Anthony Blake Photo Library/ Gerrit Buntrock: 9BR; J. Allan Cash Limited: 26BL; Bruce Coleman Limited/Gene Ahrens: 7TR; Pete Gardner: 6CR, 6BL, 7CL, 21BL; Robert Harding Picture Library: 25BR;The Image Bank: 11BR, 22BL; Oxford Scientific Films/Michael Ogden: 27BL;

Photos Horticultural/ Michael & Lois Warren: 12BR; Science Photo Library/ European Space Agency: 6TL; Seaphot Limited/Planet Earth Pictures: 13BR; Spectrum Colour Library: 15BR

Picture research Paula Cassidy and Rupert Thomas

Production Louise Barratt

Dorling Kindersley would like to thank Claire Gillard for editorial assistance; Mrs Bradbury, the staff and children of Allfarthing Junior School, Wandsworth, especially Idris Anjary, Billy Arthur, Tom Blyth, Miriam Habtesellasse, Ben Hedley, Thomas Hutchings, Mark Macleod, Anna Rimoldi and Alice Watling; Tom Armstrong.